Sweet Dreams Chicago

Adriane Doherty • Anastasiia Kuusk

Rubber Ducky Press
Indianapolis, IN

The sun rises as eager eyes open up to a new morning. We are going to explore Chicago searching for adventure.

Taking a day cruise on the Chicago River is a great way to see the city and all its beauty.
Let's go on a boat ride!

A trip to Shedd Aquarium is always an amazing day. The Caribbean Reef tank and beluga whales are two of my favorite exhibits.

The baseball park is filled with the yummy smells of cotton candy, hot buttered popcorn, and you can't forget the hotdogs. The umpire yells, "Play ball!"

A day at the beach is fun for all. The sand feels warm between our toes, and the water sparkles in the sun.

While exploring the city, the Museum of Science and Industry is a great place to visit. There are many interesting exhibits to see and science to learn. We let our imaginations go!

Another stop on our list is Navy Pier. There is so much to see and do. We walked through the Children's Museum then took a ride on the carousel. Weeeeee!

The Chicago skyline is a treasured piece of history. Everywhere we look we can see the many skyscrapers. The tallest of all is Willis Tower.

Visiting Lincoln Park Zoo is so much fun! We love seeing the giraffes, and the ostriches stretch their necks out to see what's going on.

People gather around to see the giant bean in Millennium Park. At night you can see many beautiful colors reflecting off of it. The park is a relaxing place for an evening stroll.

It's early evening as the boats begin heading back
to the docks after a long day on Lake Michigan.
Sweet dreams, boaters.

It is always a treat to go out to dinner with family. With our bellies full of Chicago-style pizza, we are ready to head home for bed.
Sweet dreams, pizza maker.

After a day of exploring, we are warm, cozy, and ready for a bedtime story.
Sweet dreams, explorers.

Wow, what a busy day.
I wonder what we'll do tomorrow.

Sweet dreams, Chicago.
Sweet dreams, everyone!

Where in Chicago did we go today?

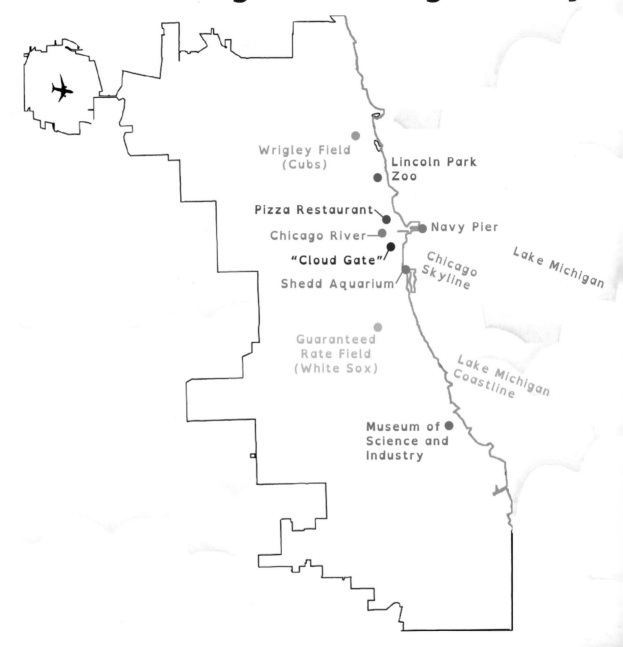

Wrigley Field
(Cubs)

Lincoln Park
Zoo

Pizza Restaurant

Chicago River

Navy Pier

"Cloud Gate"

Chicago
Skyline

Lake Michigan

Shedd Aquarium

Guaranteed
Rate Field
(White Sox)

Lake Michigan
Coastline

Museum of
Science and
Industry

e Michigan has a surface area of 404 square miles, making it the fifth-gest lake in the world.

The Chicago Skyline has five buildings over 1,000 feet tall and another eight over 800 feet tall.The tallest is Willis Tower, formerly Sears Tower, which is 1,453 feet tall, or 1,729 feet including the antenna.

edd Aquarium is home to 32,000 mals. In 1930, the Shedd transferred one ion gallons of seawater from Key West, rida.

Lincoln Park Zoo is open 365 days of the year, and there is never an admission fee. The zoo cares for hundreds of animals in state-of-the-art habitats.

Chicago River naturally emptied into e Michigan, but in 1900 the flow was ersed after eight years of construction. rn more at the McCormick Bridgehouse hicago River Museum.

The "Bean" in Millennium Park is actually the sculpture named "Cloud Gate." The Bean is 66 feet long and 33 feet high.

ording to cubsbythenumbers.com, more n 180 players have played for both the os and the White Sox baseball teams.

Chicago is the largest city on Lake Michigan, with a population of more than 2.7 million people.

cago offers two dozen beaches. Two e been designated as dog friendly— mont Harbor Beach and Montrose Beach.

Along with deep-dish and stuffed pizza, Chicago-style hot dogs are another famous food: a Vienna beef hot dog, poppy seed bun, onions, tomatoes, pickle spear, pickle relish, pickled hot peppers, and mustard.

the Museum of Science and Industry tors can board a World War II submarine a Boeing 727 inside the museum.

Abe Lincoln's first name is etched upon one of the blocks in the bedroom. Illinois claims the Civil War–era president as their own. License plates from Illinois even read "Land of Lincoln."

vy Pier first opened in 1916 as Municipal and was renamed the Navy Pier in 1927 onor of World War I Navy veterans.

Only New York and Boston have more major-league championships. Chicago has eight football, six hockey, six basketball, and six baseball championships.

Adriane Doherty

Adriane Doherty read to her young children daily, and her love of books and helping young minds grow and understand the places around them inspired her to write. Adriane has explored the city of Chicago from O'Hare Airport to Shedd Aquarium to the Museum of Science and Industry and many places in between.

Other Rubber Ducky Press Titles You May Enjoy:

ABC Christmas	ABC Texas	Sweet Dreams Indiana
ABC Indiana	ABC Yellowstone	Sweet Dreams Ohio
ABC Michigan	Sweet Dreams Chesapeake Bay	Goodnight Sleeping Bear
ABC Ohio		

Find coloring pages and puzzles at rubberduckypress.com